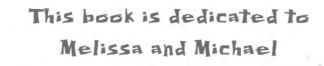

This book is dedicated to
Melissa and Michael

Copyright © 2009 by Jim Arnosky
All rights reserved. Published by Scholastic Press, an imprint of Scholastic Inc., *Publishers since 1920.* SCHOLASTIC,
SCHOLASTIC PRESS, and associated logos are trademarks and/or registered trademarks of Scholastic Inc.

BOEING® is a registered trademark of Boeing Management Company. Used without authorization.

Library of Congress Cataloging-in-Publication Data
Arnosky, Jim.
I'm a turkey! / by Jim Arnosky.—1st ed. p. cm.
Summary: In spoken-word song with rhyming text, a turkey describes his life in a large flock, always looking out for other
creatures that might find him tasty. (Internet component includes downloadable song)—Provided by publisher
ISBN-13: 978-0-439-90364-6 (hardcover) • ISBN-10: 0-439-90364-5 (hardcover)
[1. Stories in rhyme. 2. Turkeys—Fiction.] I. Title. II. Title: I am a turkey!
PZ8.3.A648Im 2009 • [E]—dc22 • 2008038335

10 9 8 7 6 5 4 3 2 1   09 10 11 12 13
Printed in Singapore 46 • First Edition, September 2009

The display type was set in Thwack. The text was set in Thud.
The art was created using acrylic paint in a semitranslucent style on acid-free watercolor paper.
Book design by Edward Miller

Download this song from the Internet at www.scholastic.com/Arnosky

I'M A TURKEY!

Jim Arnosky

Scholastic Press · New York

I got a turkey **dad** and a turkey **MoM**.

and **SISTER**, too.

I'm part of a flock of **102** –

Wild turkeys.

Every one.

When
you live
in a flock
of that
many
birds,

You've got to communicate, but not with words.

A great big

bird weighing

fifteen pounds

takes some time getting off the ground.

I flap my wings and

aim toward heaven

and take off slowly

like a Boeing . . .

747 . . .

Fifty miles per hour . . .

...Over the treetops.

You know being a **turkey** has its **UPS** and **downs**. We're **big** and **strong**,

But we must be **careful**,
can't be **hasty**,
'cuz lots of **critters**
find us . . .

Always on the lookout.

But not to **Worry**,

we keep **Surviving**,

And our numbers keep on **MULTIPLYING.**

The very next Turkey that you see
might be from my flock.

It might be Me!

Make a **gobbling** sound so I know it's you.

I'll answer back with a **gobble** or two.